COPING™

I0901543

COPING WITH STRESS

Elissa Thompson and Linda Bickerstaff

Rosen YA™
New York

Published in 2020 by The Rosen Publishing Group, Inc.
29 East 21st Street, New York, NY 10010

First Edition

Library of Congress Cataloging-in-Publication Data

Names: Thompson, Elissa, author. | Bickerstaff, Linda, author.
Title: Coping with stress / Elissa Thompson and Linda Bickerstaff.
Description: New York : Rosen Publishing, 2020 | Series: Coping | Audience: Grades 7–12. | Includes bibliographical references and index.
Identifiers: LCCN 2018050657| ISBN 9781508187257 (library bound) | ISBN 9781508187240 (pbk.)
Subjects: LCSH: Stress in adolescence—Juvenile literature. | Stress management—Juvenile literature.
Classification: LCC BF724.3.S86 T46 2019 | DDC 155.9/042—dc23
LC record available at https://lccn.loc.gov/2018050657

Manufactured in the United States of America

Many teens say school is a big cause of stress in their lives. There is a lot of worry about getting into college, which can cause added pressure to do well on papers and exams.

All these worries can be difficult to handle. "It's hard to describe the stress," Tommy La Guardia told *Time's* Schrobsdorff. "I'm calm on the outside, but inside it's like a demon in your stomach trying to consume you." Tommy doesn't like to worry his mom, though, so he doesn't like to talk about his stress with her. "I don't want to make it someone else's problem."

College life can also be a cause of stress, as living away from home for the first time, combined with new responsibilities, can weigh on students.

Add to this that much of what teens are dealing with today is new, so adults don't always know how to help. Parents didn't have smart phones growing up—there was no Facebook or Instagram, cyberbullying or Internet trolls, which can definitely contribute to teen stress.

"If you wanted to create an environment to churn out really angsty people, we've done it," Janis Whitlock, director of the Cornell Research Program on Self-Injury and Recovery, told *Time's* Schrobsdorff. "It's that they're in a cauldron of stimulus they can't get away from, or don't want to get away from, or don't know how to get away from," she said.

All of this means that stress and anxiety rates are on the rise. The *New York Times* reported that the Higher Education Research Institute at UCLA found 41 percent of incoming freshman "feel overwhelmed" by their workloads, which is more than double the number of overloaded students in 1985.

It's important to remember that everyone gets stressed sometimes. It's a natural physiological reaction, and there are ways to control those

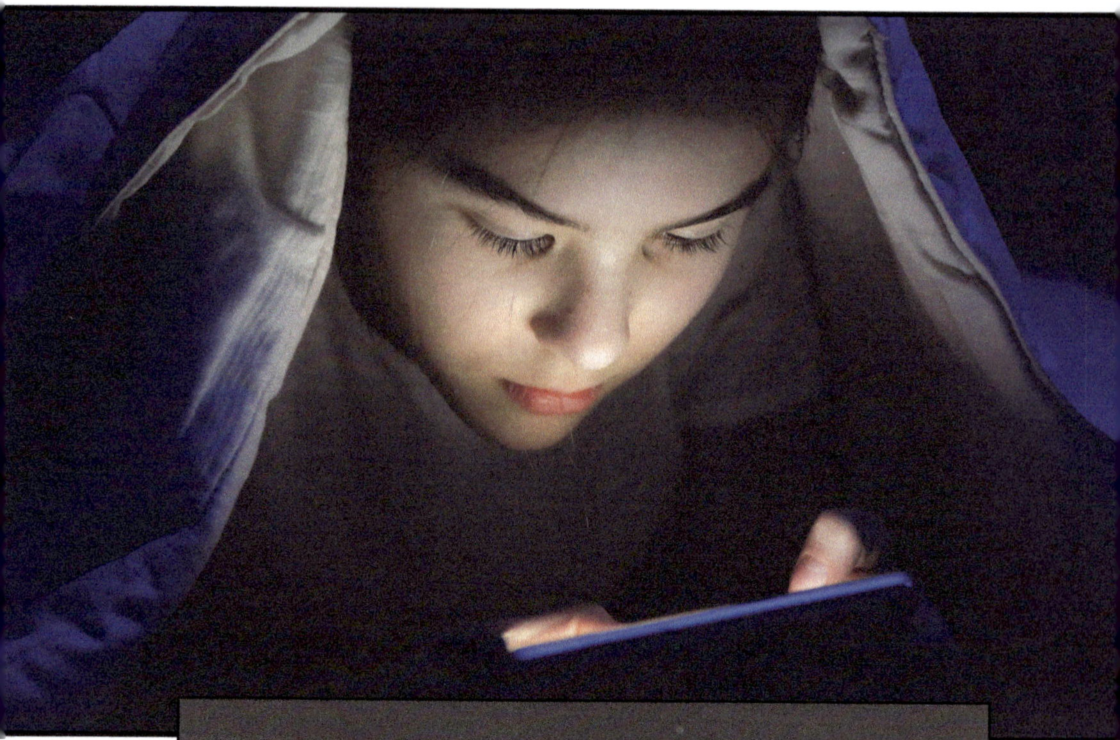

Smartphones can be very stressful for teens—especially those who aren't good at setting limits on usage. Looking at a smartphone at night can impede sleep—another stressor.

overwhelming, panicked feelings. By understanding what happens in the body when stressed—both good and bad—you can decipher what is going on inside you, learn positive coping mechanisms, and discover what stressors affect you and how to handle them. Avoiding negative stimuli and learning self-care can also help.

Let's get destressed!

CHAPTER ONE

Stress and the Body

Stress happens to everyone every day. But this is not necessarily a bad thing! Stress reactions can help one respond to changes in our environment each day. But too many stressors can be overwhelming. You may wind up feeling stressed out.

Stress 101

The word "stress" was coined when Hans Selye and another physician, Walter Bradford Cannon, began to publish the results of their research efforts back in the late ninteenth to early twentieth centuries.

In his autobiography, *The Way of an Investigator*, Dr. Cannon theorized that when presented with severe stress, the body shuts down certain functions, like digestion, which aren't needed in life-or-death situations. By doing this, blood can move to parts of the body, including the brain, heart, lungs, and muscles, where it is needed immediately. Thus, the concept of the fight-or-flight response was born.

Dr. Stress

Dr. Hans Selye was known as "Dr. Stress" in medical circles because of his contributions to understanding the effects of stress on humans. Dr. Selye differentiated between good stress and bad stress.

Good stress, which he called *eustress*, is comprised of bodily responses to stressors that help protect one in times of danger. Eustress gears up the body to study for exams, to meet deadlines—basically, to stay on one's toes in order to meet life's challenges. Eustress allows the body to return to an unstressed state within a short interval of time.

Bad stress, which Dr. Selye called *distress*, is the result of too much of a good thing. Stress responses are automatic, and one can't do anything to stop them from occurring. If a person is constantly being stressed, his or her body's stress reactions will begin to overlap. Temporary bodily changes, like elevated blood pressure and heart rate, may become present all the time. This can contribute to the development of very significant health problems, including heart attacks and strokes.

Dr. Hans Selye is considered the father of the field of stress. He was a respected endocrinologist whose contributions to the study of stress still help researchers today.

How Stress Affects the Body

It's impossible to go through an entire day without encountering stressors and reacting to them. Regardless of what the stressor is, the body will react the same way every time it is stressed. Here's what happens:

- **Heart rate, respiratory rate, and blood pressure increase**. At the same time, blood flow to the skin, digestive system, and kidneys decreases. As a result, more blood is shunted to organs, like the lungs, brain, and large muscle groups, which really need it in emergency situations. When blood flow is increased to the brain, its ability to respond quickly to stressors improves. Increased blood flow to large muscle groups enables one to flee from a perceived danger.
- **Sweating increases.** The chemical reactions occurring in the body in response to stress create a lot of body heat. Increased sweating helps the body eliminate this extra heat.
- **The pupils dilate or enlarge.** When the pupils dilate, they allow more light into the eyes to improve vision.

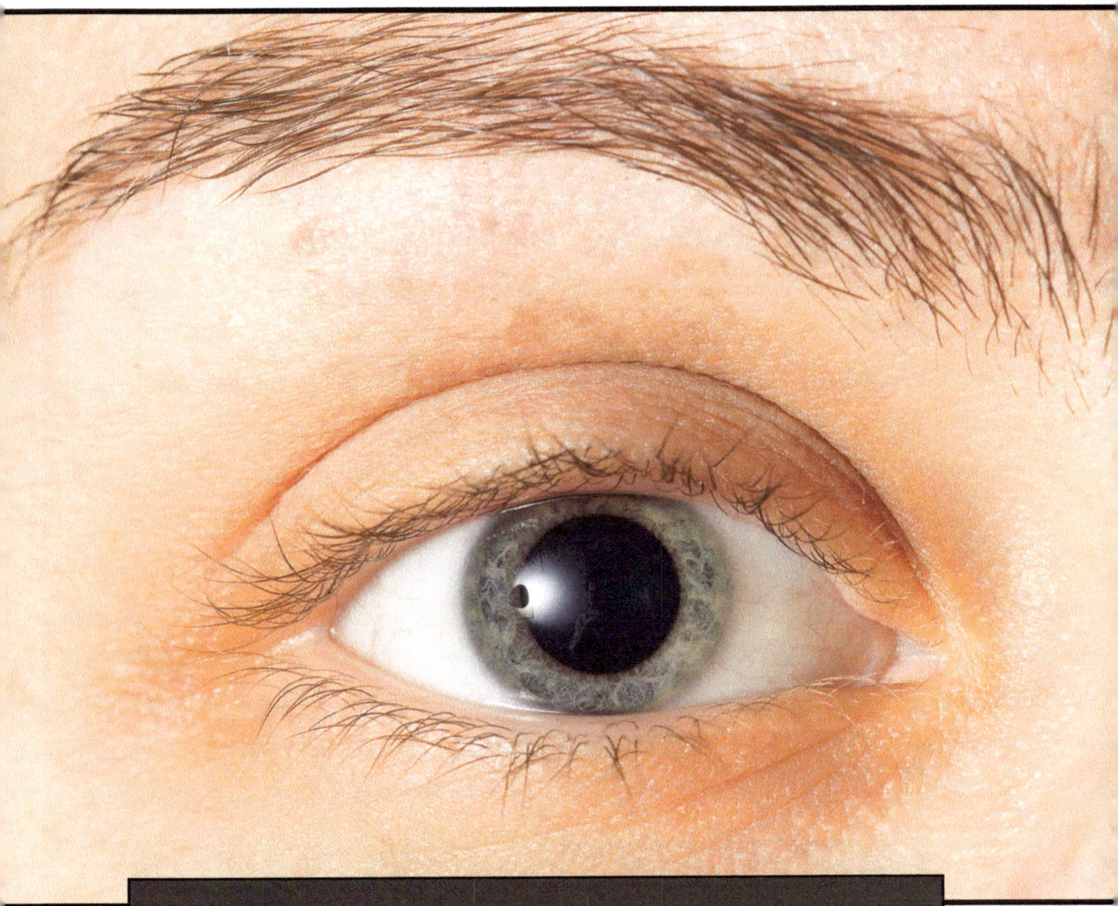

When the body is stressed, it does several things to help itself get out of perceived danger. This includes pupil dilation, which improves vision and can assist in survival.

- **Stored glycogen is released from the liver.** When undergoing a stress reaction, the body needs a lot of extra energy to fuel its systems. The body's energy source is glucose, a form of sugar. The liver, which stores sugar as glycogen, releases it in response to stress.

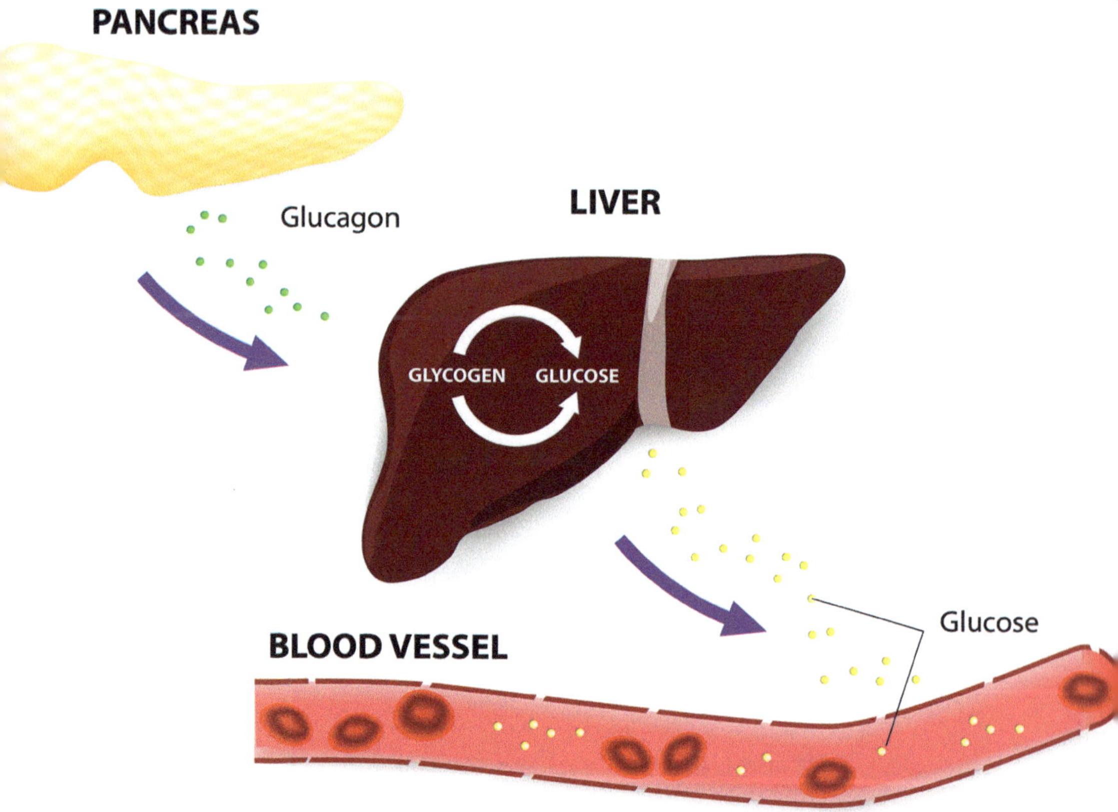

When the body's glucose level becomes too low, the pancreas releases glucagon. Glucagon makes the liver convert glycogen into glucose, which is let into the bloodstream.

- **Stored platelets and clotting factors release.** If one gets a cut on their finger, platelets, or small particles that circulate in the bloodstream, cause a chemical reaction that makes blood clot at the site of the cut. In a stress reaction, large numbers of platelets, which are stored in bone marrow, are sent out into the circulating blood. At the same time, chemicals called clotting factors, which are also necessary for blood clotting, are moved out of storage into the bloodstream to speed up the clotting mechanism if it is needed.

Physiology of Stress

When stressed, a series of reactions are kicked off within the body. Let's say you step off the curb onto the street while distracted, not noticing an oncoming car. Here is what happens:

1. The screech of the brakes travels to your ears, where it causes your eardrums to vibrate. The three bones of the middle ear carry those vibrations to nerve cells in your inner ears. There, they are converted to electrical impulses. From there, your auditory nerves carry these impulses to your brain.
2. The impulses travel deep into the brain to the hypothalamus. Here, cells begin to make a hormone called corticotropin-releasing hormone (CRH).

3. CRH is dumped into the blood and carried through small veins to your pituitary gland. Once CRH reaches the pituitary gland, it acts on the gland's cells and causes them to make another hormone called adrenocorticotropic hormone (ACTH).
4. ACTH is absorbed into the blood and carried all the way from the head to the adrenal glands, two clumps of tissue located just above the kidneys. There, ACTH causes cells of the adrenal glands to produce three hormones: cortisol, epinephrine, and norepinephrine.
5. The three hormones travel through the bloodstream to different places in your body. Cortisol goes to your liver, where it pushes glucose that is stored there into the blood. The glucose is then carried to organs that need it. Epinephrine and norepinephrine travel all over your body to stimulate your autonomic nervous system, which helps control the body during an emergency. Thanks to the epinephrine, your heart rate soars, and your blood pressure can shoot up, too.

A car careens toward you as you step into a crosswalk and your body's stress reaction snaps into action. This helps you to quickly and safely scramble back onto the curb.

6. After you scramble back onto the curb unharmed, your stress reaction begins to subside. The reaction is turned off when you no longer need all the cortisol your adrenal glands are producing. The extra cortisol is carried back to the brain where it stops the

hypothalamus from producing CRH. This is called a feedback mechanism, and it is one of the ways the body turns off reactions it no longer needs.

The Cycle of Stress

Dr. Selye discovered that stress causes a three-stage pattern of response that he called the general adaptation syndrome (GAD), which is what happens to a body when it is stressed.

1. **The Alarm Stage:** When you stepped off the curb, you sensed a threat and your body responded to allow you to get back to the curb unharmed. After the car passed, your body's stress reaction was turned off and your physiologic parameters, like heart rate and blood pressure, started to return to normal.
2. **The Adaptive/Resistance Stage:** As you continue your walk down the street, you again hear screeching brakes. Although you are no longer in harm's way, you experience another

stress reaction. However, your heart rate and blood pressure are not as high as with your first reaction.

3. **The Exhaustion Stage:** If you experience unrelenting stress, you may reach a point where you can no longer elicit a stress response.

Myths & FACTS

Myth: Everyone deals with stress the same way.

Fact: Dr. George Chrousos, UNESCO Chair on Adolescent Health Care at the University of Athens, believes that stress responses vary from person to person. One may overeat, or not eat at all. One could become argumentative or abusive, neglect personal hygiene, withdraw from friends, or start performing poorly in school. One may even go so far as to start using drugs or alcohol. Recognizing your unique stressors and how you respond to them, as well as understanding what is really happening in your body when you are stressed, are the beginning steps in learning to control stress.

Myth: Genetics don't matter when it comes to stress.

Fact: A person's genetic makeup may influence his or her stress response. One might fail to have strong enough responses to a threat, while someone else might over-respond to even minor stressors. Each of these variants can lead to long-term health problems.

Myth: Childhood stress doesn't affect you later on.

Fact: Extreme stress at any given time in one's life can alter the brain's hormone production, leading to possible extreme responses. If a young child experiences extreme stress, he or she may overreact to even minor stress as an adult.

CHAPTER TWO

Stress Can Make You Sick

Have you ever experienced stress overload? Then you know how bad it can make you feel. Scientists now say that if you are stressed all the time, it can have negative effects on your body. Being stressed constantly can increase your risk of high blood pressure, anxiety, and other conditions.

Stress and Immunity

The body's immune system is responsible for protecting it from foreign invaders such as bacteria or viruses. When the immune system kicks into gear, immune molecules coordinate an attack on foreign invaders.

Immune molecules can activate the hypothalamus, starting a typical stress reaction

Ever felt run down right around finals? This is because stress overload can overtax your immune system. The result? You end up sick!

that results in the production of cortisol by the adrenal glands. Cortisol has the effect of making immune cells less effective in fighting invaders.

Overstressed people have consistently high levels of cortisol, and as a result, their immune systems are more susceptible to colds, the flu, or other infections.

Have you ever developed a fever blister or cold sore on your lip just before a big event like the prom? These lesions are symptoms of herpes simplex, which is caused by a virus that can lie dormant in nerve tissue for years. Physical or emotional stress with immune system suppression is one of the most common causes of a new outcropping of blisters.

Gastrointestinal Trouble

Stomach aches before exams or a big game? Stress can also affect digestion and the gastrointestinal system.

Peptic ulcers: A peptic ulcer is an area in the stomach or the first portion of the small intestine, the duodenum, where the normal lining of these organs, the mucosa, has been worn away. This hole in the mucosa allows the contents of the stomach, which contain a large amount of acid, to penetrate into the underlying muscles.

People with peptic ulcers have been shown to have large quantities of *H. pylori*, a common bacterium found in the human body, in their stomachs. *H. pylori* may multiply in the stomachs of these individuals because their immune systems cannot fight the bacteria off. As a result, they develop ulcers. There are many factors that contribute to ulcer formation, but inability to cope with stress compounds the problem.

Irritable bowel syndrome (IBS): IBS is what doctors call a "gut-brain interaction," and can cause abdominal pain, constipation, and diarrhea—or a mix of all three symptoms. Scientists at the National Institute of Diabetes and Digestive and Kidney Diseases believe IBS can be caused by food moving too slowly or quickly through your digestive system thanks to genetics, stress, or an infection.

High Blood Pressure

Hypertension, or high blood pressure, is one of the main culprits in the development of atherosclerosis, a hardening of the arteries, which can lead to heart attacks and strokes. At least seventy-five million, or one in three, American adults are hypertensive, according to the Centers for Disease Control and

Prevention. And Sandra L. Jackson's scientific journal article in the *Morbidity and Mortality Weekly Report* says that 4 percent of teens have hypertension as well. Heart disease, including heart attacks and strokes, are the number-one killer of people in the United States, according to the CDC's "Mortality in the United States 2016."

Remember how epinephrine released in stress responses causes elevations in blood pressure and heart rate? In stress overload, large amounts of epinephrine are present in the circulatory system

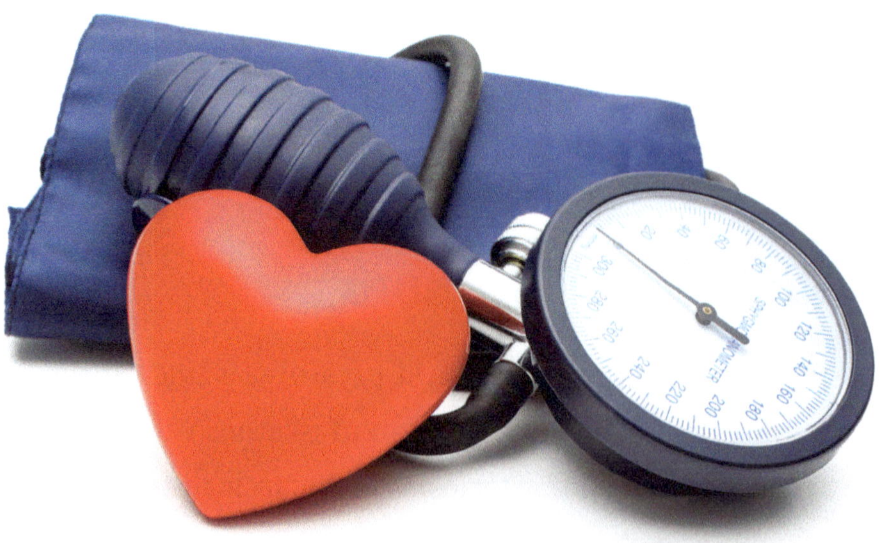

Too much stress can have a negative effect on blood pressure and can cause long-term health problems if it is not managed correctly.

all the time. This causes very high blood pressure, especially in people who have inherited the tendency to develop hypertension. People who are overweight or who have high cholesterol levels are also at special risk to develop hypertension.

The Doctor Is In

Stress can make it hard for your immune system to respond correctly, which means it can make you sick. But how do you know if you've got a serious illness or just a bug? For example, the upset stomach you may occasionally get when you are worried about taking a test is not a symptom of the development of an ulcer. But if stress controls your life and you don't find productive ways to cope with it, you might be setting yourself up for problems. If your stomach ache persists or your sadness or worry begins interfering in your everyday life, it's time to let an adult know and get yourself to a doctor. Talking to your parents, school nurse, or counselor might be the first step

(continued on the next page)

(continued from the previous page)

in learning how to handle your stress. There are many ways to help cope with stress, but you have to start by asking for help!

Medical professionals, like doctors and nurses, can have great ideas on how to manage stress. Consider talking with someone if your stress level begins to feel overwhelming.

Weight

According to the CDC, nearly one in five children from ages six to nineteen is obese, an amount that has tripled since the 1970s. Obesity is caused by many factors, including genetics and diet. Medical researchers are still working to find out how to combat obesity. But researchers do know that people who are stressed out produce large amounts of cortisol, and cortisol is known to increase appetite, which can cause weight gain.

Feelings of Sadness and Suicide

Some types of depression are characterized by anxiety, rapid heart rate, and high blood pressure, among other things. Do these signs sound familiar? These are the same signs found in stress reactions. In this disorder, the feedback mechanism for turning off CRH, the corticotropin-releasing hormone, does not work. Someone who develops depression when overstressed may do so because they are genetically programmed to produce too much CRH. In an apparent attempt to turn off CRH production, the body produces a lot of cortisol, but a side effect of having high levels of cortisol in your blood is depression.

While not all types of depression are associated with high cortisol levels, depression is a frequent symptom seen in kids who are stressed out. When people feel that they can no longer cope with a stressful situation, they might think the only option is to escape from the situation by committing suicide.

The teen suicide rate has increased 70 percent between 2006 and 2016, according to a report by Dr. Holly Hedegaard at the Centers for Disease Control and Prevention. Suicide is the second leading cause of death among adolescents and young adults fifteen to twenty-four years of age. And the suicide rate for teens is on the rise, increasing 56 percent between 2007 and 2016, according to a report from the Centers for Disease Control and Prevention.

Most teens who attempt suicide do so to escape from extremely stressful situations that seem impossible to deal with in any other way. Teens who have had a family member or a close friend commit suicide are more likely to attempt suicide. A recent death in the family is another predisposing factor. Substance abuse is also associated with suicides and suicide attempts. Alcohol and some drugs have depressive effects on the brain. Teens who are stressed and depressed may turn to alcohol and drugs to escape their symptoms, only to find that they are even more depressed. Alcohol and drugs impair a person's ability to assess risks, make good choices, and think of solutions to problems.

Not all suicides are planned. A suicide attempt is a call for help. Many teens have trouble telling their parents and friends how they feel. One may look at attempting suicide as a way of letting people know that they are hurting. Unfortunately, what starts out as an attempt may end in death—a terrible solution to a temporary problem.

If you are experiencing significant depression and think there are no solutions to your problems, talk to someone about how you feel before your depression deepens to the point where you are unable to ask for help. If you feel like you can't talk with your parents, remember that hotlines are available in almost every

NATIONAL
SUICIDE
PREVENTION
LIFELINE™
1-800-273-TALK (8255)
suicidepreventionlifeline.org

If you are considering suicide, please talk to someone you love or call the National Suicide Prevention Lifeline. Someone is available to talk twenty-four hours a day, seven days a week.

community in the country, and there are also national toll-free numbers that you can call to get help. The key is to talk to someone. If you are considering suicide, you need to get help immediately. Tell an adult or call the National Suicide Prevention Lifeline at (800) 273-8255.

Anxiety

Anxiety can be caused by the release of cortisol and adrenaline, hormones present when the body is stressed. Anxiety symptoms can also include racing heartbeat, hyperventilation, sleep problems, and more. Sometimes someone who has anxiety might even suffer a panic attack, a sudden feeling of intense fear when there is no real danger. If you have a panic attack, tell an adult and see a doctor for help right away.

Other Concerns

Extreme, long-term stress can cause other difficulties in the body as well. Here are two additional complications that can come from experiencing a lot of stress.

Reproductive malfunctions. Teens who are significantly stressed out have high amounts of cortisol circulating in their bloodstreams. In girls, this keeps ovaries from releasing eggs, and in boys, it keeps testes from releasing sperm. The production of testosterone, estrogen, and progesterone (sex hormones) is also impaired. Adult ballerinas and long-distance runners are examples of people who commonly have physical stress. These individuals, like teens with significant stress, are also known to have very high circulating cortisol levels. They have reproductive system malfunctions that can last for several years after they cease dancing or running.

Delayed growth. Children who are emotionally and physically abused at a young age can experience growth retardation. Their pituitary glands produce a lot of ACTH, adrenocorticotropic hormone, which produces cortisol in response to stress—at the expense of the production of growth hormone. If these children are placed in caring environments and receive sufficient positive attention, thereby reducing their stress levels, their growth will resume.

These are just a few examples of the effects of stress and overstress on the body. Too much stress can lead to diseases and disorders that can not only shorten life but also make the process of living difficult.

CHAPTER THREE

Being a Teen Is Stressful

Being a teen can be stressful—you know that! You have to deal with school, friends, relationships, social media, and more. While everyone deals with their own particular stressors, there are some issues you will have in common with other kids your age. Take heart, this means that you are not alone.

Familial Concerns

No family situation is stress-free. Even teens who are lucky enough to have caring parents and reasonable siblings are sometimes stressed by family issues. They know, however, that they can rely on family members for support. Some teens are not so lucky. The following stressors are among the hardest that teens deal with.

Sexual Abuse

Child Protective Services reported in its 2014 "Child Maltreatment Survey" that every eight minutes they either substantiate or find evidence of child sexual abuse. More than 80 percent of the time, the abuser was a parent.

Teens from abusive households may have been dealing with abuse for years. While one can adapt or cope, there will be scars—physical or emotional. Many of the coping mechanisms one might develop are negative ones. If you, a sibling, or a friend have been abused, tell a responsible adult. Talking to someone takes a great deal of courage, but it can be the only way to stop the abuse.

Divorce

Divorce can be difficult for the entire family to handle. A teen might feel guilt over the divorce, concern about younger siblings, and worry regarding living situations. Perhaps your parents divorced when you were younger, or you are facing this extremely stressful situation now. Talking with an adult who is not directly involved—a school counselor, a teacher, or even the parent of a friend—may help you get through this difficult time.

Illness and Death

A major illness or the death of a parent or sibling is extremely stressful for a teen. Dealing with grief and wanting to be supportive for the remaining family members, all while coping with the other stresses of teen life, can be overwhelming. Teens may feel that they should be the supporters when all they really want to do is be supported. Remember that everyone grieves in their own way, in their own time. Talking about your feelings with a loved one can help.

School Stress

School can be a stressful place, thanks to worries about grades, friends—and even safety. Getting into college, and concerns about expensive tuition, can also cause stress.

Parental Expectations

For many teens, living up to their parents' expectations can be extremely stressful. This is especially true if one feels these expectations are unrealistic, or if one feels the need to be as good as or better than an older sibling. Most parents want their children to succeed, and school performance is one parameter

There is a lot about adolescent life that is stressful—from schoolwork to friend trouble to relationship blues. Know that you are not alone—and you can get through it!

that a parent looks at to judge whether a child is on the right track. However, a parent's definition of the "right track" can be quite different than their teen's.

What do you do if your parents think you should pursue courses strong in the sciences, but your real interests and talents are in the arts? Conflicts like these are major stressors. They become even more significant if you can't talk to your parents about the problem or are unable to find a compromise that all of you can live with. It would be helpful to talk with a teacher or school counselor who could give you advice about the best way to deal with such conflicts.

Homework Overload and Grades Stress

The pressure to do well in school can be overwhelming. The American Psychological Association surveyed teens in 2013 and discovered they are as stressed as adults! Robin H. Gurwitch, professor and clinical psychologist at Duke University Medical Center, told *People* magazine's Julie Mazziotta, "The most common reports of stress among teens is in school, followed only by stress related to 'what am I going to do after high school,' and 'will I get into the colleges that I want.'"

And then there's homework. A 2015 study by New York University's College of Nursing found that students at some private schools do up to three hours of homework a night, and that's after extracurricular activities and jobs.

"School, homework, extracurricular activities, sleep, repeat—that's what it can be for some of these students," says Noelle Leonard, a senior research scientist at the New York University College of Nursing (NYUCN). This type of schedule can lead to chronic stress, which can cause health problems.

It can be stressful worrying about getting homework done. It can be even more stressful worrying about getting the best grades to get into the best college to get the best job, but try to maintain some perspective. One bad grade is not going to ruin your chances of having a nice life. If you're feeling overwhelmed by your schoolwork or discouraged by your grades, try talking to your teacher, school counselor, or parent. They might be able to help.

Activity Overload

High school counselors often say that it takes more than grades for a teen to get into a good college or university. The question is: How much more? College admission committees check students' extracurricular activities to see if they've successfully held down jobs, done volunteer work, showed leadership skills in organizations, or developed athletic, artistic, or musical skills. These criteria give admission committee members a feel for what a student's interests are. Some teens may be carrying the push to be "well-rounded" too far. Many are packing so much into their lives that they are truly stressed out.

College admissions officers generally consider it impossible to measure or compare the quality of a student's extracurricular activities, so your chances of being admitted to a college is not necessarily enhanced by the number of extracurricular activities you report. Nevertheless, teens are being overwhelmed by the demands on their time.

Learning to diplomatically say "no" is difficult, but it is perhaps one of the greatest skills one can learn.

College Concerns

Getting into college is a big deal for many teens, and it causes a lot of stress. Worrying about having the best application—and concern over how to pay for skyrocketing tuition—can be difficult for a teen to handle.

Sometimes teens put pressure on themselves regarding college and don't let their parents know what they're experiencing. College is a big and expensive life step. It's important, yes, but it won't decide everything about your life. Talk it over with your parent or a trusted adult.

School Shootings

School shootings are a big fear—and source of stress—for teens. More than 57 percent of teens say they are worried about a shooting happening at their school, according to an article by Nikki Graf for the Pew Research Center.

If you are scared about a school shooting, talk with an adult you trust, make a hotline call, or seek out a

Flowers and cards were placed outside Marjory Stoneman Douglas High School in Parkland, Florida. A deadly shooting there on February 14, 2018, killed seventeen people.

friend for some help. There are ways to stay safe, to understand the likelihood of something happening at your school, and to create positive change.

Peer Pressure

For some teens, having one or two good friends to hang out with is all they need to be comfortable. Others want to fit into and be accepted by a larger group. Regardless of how many people make up your peer group, their opinions are probably very important. Your friend group can have an incredible amount of influence on you. Decisions about whether or not to go along with the crowd will have to be made on many occasions. These decisions may be difficult and stressful to make.

Dating

It is not unusual for both members of a couple to be very busy with school, sports, and work. In this instance, they frequently feel that they have to "steal" time to be with each other. In some cases, one partner is busier than the other. The less busy partner feels that he or she comes second place to everything else—a very stressful situation for both members of the couple.

Dating violence, defined as the intentional use of abusive tactics in order to obtain and maintain control over an intimate partner, can also be a major

Teen relationships can be new and exciting experiences. They can also cause stress as adolescents navigate sex and romantic love for the first time.

stressor for some teens. According to the National Center for Injury Prevention and Control at the CDC, one out of nine teenage girls and one in thirteen teen boys reported experiencing sexual violence in the past year. The abuse can range from threats to stalking to physical and sexual violence. Dating violence can be one incident in which a person was date raped or repeated physical abuse that some teens endure because they mistakenly believe that their partner loves them and is using physically abusive sex "for their own good." Dating violence may start at an early age. According to the CDC, 23 percent of women and 14 percent of men report having experienced sexual violence before the age of eighteen.

Dating violence should be reported to a responsible adult, but it can be difficult for victims to feel comfortable doing so. Victims often feel that they allowed the violence to happen so it is their own fault, or their abusers may have blamed them. Whatever the reason, if you are the victim of sexual violence, you are not responsible. It is not your fault.

Because victims of date rape or dating violence have difficulty in taking steps to stop the violence, most communities have established hotlines. These are call centers that are manned 24/7 to provide initial help to those who need it. If you are a victim of dating violence, help is a phone call or a text away.

Bullying

The term *bullying* is used to describe a variety of different behaviors, such as teasing, name calling, intentionally not inviting someone to a social event, ignoring someone, or gossiping about him/her. At its extreme, bullying can also involve physical contact, like hitting, pinching, pushing, slapping, or other forms of assault.

In 2018, a study by the National Center for Education Statistics found that about 21 percent of students, ages twelve to eighteen, reported being bullied.

As with dating violence, you need to let someone know if you are being bullied. When bullying occurs in schools, alerting a teacher or counselor would be a positive first step. Many schools have rules in place to try and deal with bullying. Hotlines are also available to provide help for those being bullied. Since many who are bullied become bullies, getting help early is important to avoid long-term problems.

Gangs Are Not the Answer

Some teens join gangs to gain protection from others who are harassing or threatening them, or to have a sense of family. Today's gangs are groups of teens and young adults who hang out together and are often involved in violent or criminal activities. Youth gangs are often organized and controlled by adult criminal leaders who use members of the gang to do their dirty work.

For most teens who actually join gangs, membership is usually brief: a study done by Sam Houston State University in 2015 found that four hundred thousand kids join gangs each year—while four hundred thousand also leave gangs. "Being a gang member is not all that it is cracked up to be, which is something kids realize once they get involved and find out that the money, cars, girls, and protection is more myth than reality," said David Pyrooz, assistant professor of criminal justice at Sam Houston State University.

Stressors at home can make kids turn to gangs. The gang members become their new family, forging a very strong bond. These teens can come from homes where they have been physically and emotionally abused. They join gangs to get away from what they perceive to be excessive parental control. By doing so, they place themselves in the position of being used by the adults who organize and direct gangs. Gang members can be plied with alcohol and drugs, and they do all the work, take all the risks, and are totally expendable.

Kids who join gangs are usually doing so to try to escape some of the significant stressors in their lives. Unfortunately, in doing so, they create a new set of problems that may be much more serious than those they wish to escape.

Self-Image

The way you perceive yourself may be closely tied to your peer group. It is not uncommon to want to be as attractive and outgoing as the most popular student in school. And then there's social media, television, and more bombarding everyone with picture-perfect images of women and men who look flawless.

Remember that no one looks perfect all the time. Learning to live in your own skin is very hard to do, especially if you feel that your appearance is keeping you from being accepted by your peers. Makeup, tattoos, and body piercings are different ways that teens try to improve their self-image. If you are having a difficult time accepting your appearance, consider talking with your parent or a doctor. There are many professionals available to help you work through self-image issues.

The Internet

Any teen today will probably tell you that the internet is both terrible and wonderful. It's a great way to chat with friends, to follow musicians and actors, and to find out the answer to so many things. But the internet can also be a seriously stressful place.

Cyberbullying

Cyberbullying involves verbal harassment, rumor spreading, and the release of private information.

About 34 percent of students report being cyberbullied, according to a 2015 report by Justin W. Patchin for the Cyberbullying Research Center. Many schools have anticyberbullying policies. In California, schools are required to have systems in place to quickly address bullying. This is because of California's 2011 Seth's Law, named after thirteen-year-old Seth Walsh, who committed suicide after being bullied about his sexual orientation.

Cyberbullying can cause a great amount of stress. But there are things you can do to stop someone from bullying you online. Your first step may be to talk to a trusted adult, parent, teacher, or counselor. They can help.

Social Media Stress

How many likes did that picture get? Was everyone at that party but you? Social media can cause a lot of stress in a teen's life.

One way to combat social media stress is to put down the phone. If you can limit your screen access, your feelings may improve. Some things you can do? Hang out with friends in person, play a sport, read a print copy of a book or magazine, and consider going to church if you are religious. If social media is stressing you out, why not try one of those activities instead? And resist the urge to pick up your phone and post about it.

Current Events

The world can seem like a scary place. Worries about politics, the environment, the economy, and more can definitely stress a teen out. National and world issues are especially potent stressors because most teens feel there is nothing they can do about them. Not so! There is plenty a teen can do *right now.* Become active in groups working to combat racism, change gun laws, or protest

Emma González speaks at the Washington, DC, March For Our Lives on March 24, 2018. She has become an inspiring spokesperson for gun control.

Pakistani social leader Malala Yousafzai won the Nobel Peace Prize in 2014. She was seventeen years old, the youngest recipient ever to receive the award.

climate change. Trying to cause positive change is a great way to relieve stress.

Teen activists like Emma González are trying to make a difference now. They aren't waiting until they are older. González survived the school shooting at Marjory Stoneman Douglas High School in Parkland, Florida. She is now famous for speaking out about the importance of gun control. Malala Yousafzai is an activist for human rights and female education. She is the youngest person to ever win a Nobel Prize. Then there's Thandiwe Abdullah, who helped found the Black Lives Matter Youth Vanguard movement, to fight against racial profiling and police violence. These teens are working to make the world a better place by fighting for causes they believe in. You can do this, too. You are in a position to directly affect national and world events in the future.

CHAPTER FOUR

Increasing Stress

Often it is possible to cope with stress. You can do some yoga. Talk with your mom or best friend. But sometimes, stress can completely overwhelm you. You might want to try drugs or alcohol to escape your problems. But truly, these negative coping mechanisms will only create more problems in the long run. Here are some self-destructive coping mechanisms.

Addiction

Addiction is a condition in which your life is being controlled by some habit. Addiction is

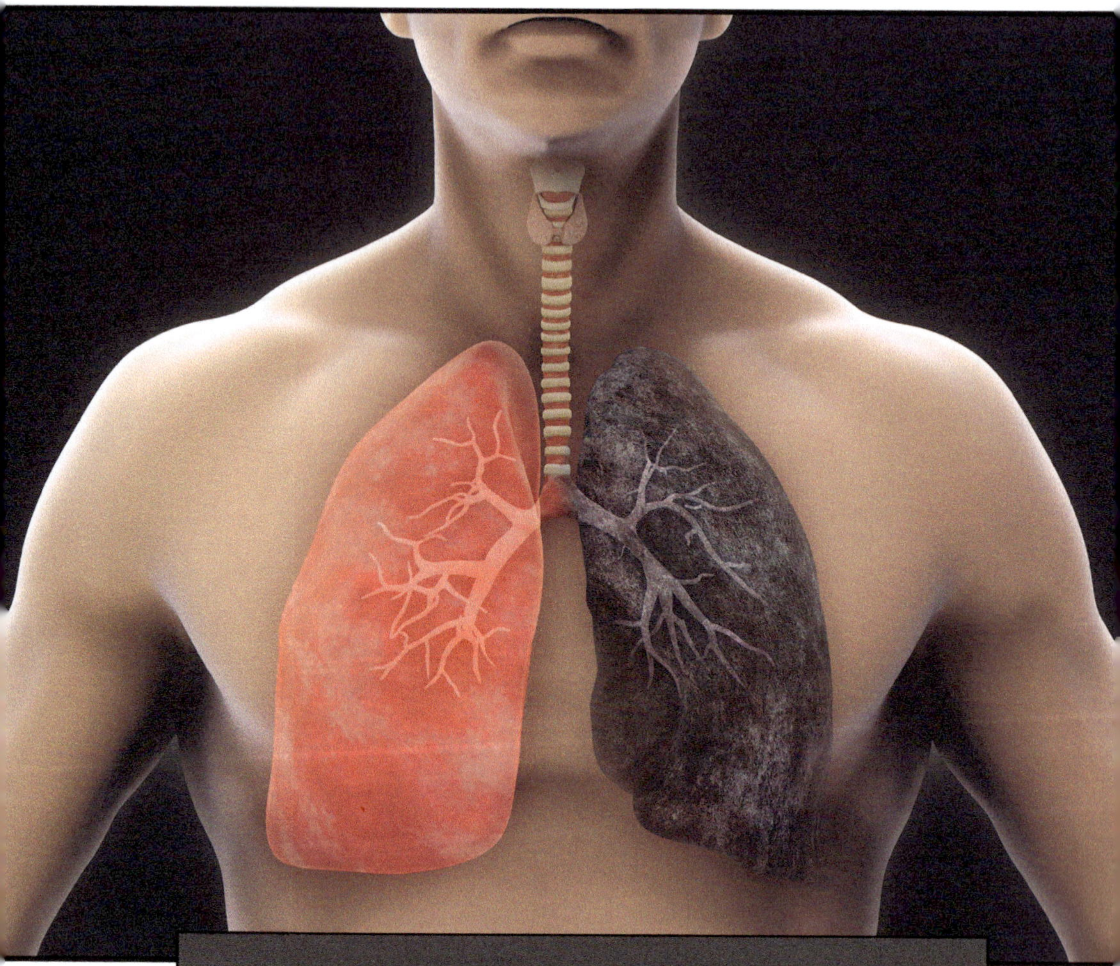

While some say they smoke to destress, smoking has a very negative effect on the body. Becoming addicted to nicotine can definitely add stress to one's life.

sometimes refered to as a craving, an enslavement, and a dependence. Smoking, drinking, drug use, and gambling are examples of habits or behaviors that teens use to try to cope with the stressors in their lives. All of them can, and frequently do, become addictions.

Smoking

Tobacco use is an addiction. Nicotine is the addictive drug in tobacco that users need more and more of. The development of addiction to tobacco is a complex, learned process that involves actual physical changes in the body of the person as they experiment with tobacco use. The habit becomes integrated into a smoker's daily activities and may actually control those activities. For example, because it is illegal to smoke on airplanes, heavy smokers may think twice about taking nonstop flights that last longer than three to four hours.

For many teens, smoking is a way of dealing with their stressful worlds. In the long run, however, it will only make things worse. And the teen years are when tobacco addiction typically takes hold. According to a 2018 study on drug use, Monitoring Future National Survey Results on Drug Use 1975–2017, nine out of ten tobacco users start before they are eighteen years old. Eleven percent of high school seniors reported having had a cigarette in the past month. But there is good news: cigarette smoking is on the decline. Daily reported use of tobacco products by high school seniors has gone from 24.6 percent in 1997 to 4.2 in 2017. That is great news.

While most kids today are aware that smoking can lead to major health problems, there are still those who begin smoking—and it will be very difficult for them to stop. A 2014 report from the surgeon general estimates that if current smoking rates among teens continue, 5.6 million of them will die prematurely from a smoking-related disease. That's about one in thirteen teens alive today!

Although nicotine is a very dangerous drug and is extremely addictive, its drug effect has been described as "mild." It doesn't take long for the body of a smoker to adapt to the drug, so smokers need to smoke more and more to get the same buzz they originally got with just a few cigarettes. Smoking is not a way to deal with stress. Instead, it will probably end up giving you more things to be stressed about in the future.

Vaping 101

While adolescent smoking rates are down, teens are beginning to increase their use of e-vaporizers. According to the Monitoring the Future 2017 survey, nearly one in three high school seniors report having used e-vaporizers in the past year.

So what is vaping? Generally it is when one uses a battery-operated electronic device, or e-cigarette, to inhale the vapor of liquid nicotine, flavoring, or cannabis, aka marijuana. Because vaping is relatively new, researchers aren't sure of its long-term effects.

(continued on the next page)

Experts are still learning about vaping and its effects on the body. Vaping may help people trying to quit smoking. But it can also get one addicted to nicotine. So vape with caution.

(continued from the previous page)

There is more work to be done. So if you choose to vape, be aware that you can't be sure what it will do to your body.

Alcohol Abuse

Alcohol's large presence in American culture coupled with busy parents and rising rates of stress and depression among youths results in a "cocktail of reasons" explaining underage alcohol use. The stress of teen life, peer pressure, and a desire for independence contribute to teenage drinking.

A 2017 fact sheet from the National Institute on Alcohol Abuse and Alcoholism says more than 5.1 million teens have participated in binge drinking (which means five or more drinks for males or four or more drinks for females within a few hours) in the past month. Binge drinking can lead to serious problems like increased risk of physical and sexual assault, injuries, and even death. The Centers for

Disease Control and Prevention reports that alcohol plays a role in 4,358 deaths of people twenty-one and under each year. The causes? Car accidents, homicides, accidents, and suicide.

The question is, does drinking alcohol really relieve stress? When an alcoholic beverage is consumed, alcohol gets into the bloodstream in a hurry. It takes about thirty minutes before the full effects of the drink are felt, but the brain gets its first jolt within thirty seconds. Most drinkers think that alcohol relieves stress because they initially feel good after taking a drink. But alcohol isn't a stimulant, it's a depressant.

Alcohol is eliminated from the body much more slowly than it is absorbed. It takes men about one hour to eliminate or metabolize the alcohol from one drink, while it takes women slightly longer. If you spend a full hour drinking a beer or sipping a glass of wine, you may never experience its depressant effects because the alcohol is being eliminated about as rapidly as it is being consumed. However, binge drinking means alcohol is being introduced into the system much more quickly. It takes only three to four drinks within an hour for a man to be legally

There are so many ways to have fun with your friends and romantic partners without drinking alcohol, smoking cigarettes, or using other drugs.

drunk, while a woman might be legally drunk with only two drinks in an hour. A blood alcohol content of 0.08 percent is considered legally drunk in all states.

In two weeks of drinking a couple of beers a day, the body adapts to the alcohol. Then you have to increase your alcohol consumption considerably to get the high that you used to get with just two drinks. Your brain cells adapt to having alcohol in the system. Once that happens, you are addicted and may experience withdrawal symptoms if you stop drinking. These symptoms can range from mild hand tremors, stomach upset, and excessive sweating to potentially life-threatening confusion, severe depression, hallucinations, and even seizures.

Like all addictive coping mechanisms, drinking alcohol does not relieve stress—it adds to your stress level.

Drug Abuse

A teen may use drugs to deal with life stress because of peer pressure or maybe even out of curiosity or boredom. While teen use of prescription opioids and harder drugs like heroin are on the decline, according to the Monitoring Future National Survey Results on Drug Use 1975–2017, marijuana use has increased. Twenty-four percent of the 45,000 students surveyed in 380 private and public schools across the country said they had used marijuana in the past year.

Some say this increase is because marijuana is no longer viewed as risky, especially as the drug has been become legal to use in many states. But there is a larger concern for teen marijuana use, and it's that your brain isn't done developing yet. An example from the National Institute of Drug Abuse says, "The adolescent brain is often likened to a car with a fully functioning gas pedal (the reward system) but weak brakes (the prefrontal cortex)." Your brain will not be fully developed until your mid-twenties. Marijuana use can harm the organ by making it harder to pay attention, remember things, and solve problems.

Drug abuse is one step in a series of events in addictive behavior. Many who wind up addicted to drugs begin using as teens. As a teen, your brain may be telling you to try out new experiences, but it is important to be mindful of the consequences of your decisions. If you're feeling stressed, will drug use help or cause more problems?

Gambling

Have you ever gambled? Most kids gamble for fun—and many of their gambling activities are actually innocent games played at parties. Gambling is much more available now, thanks to online gambling, than it was in generations past. This means it is easier to try out gambling, but it is also easier to get addicted.

Many teens start gambling to escape stress or because they can't say no to the temptation. But once a teen starts, one can get hooked—and then it is possible to become a compulsive gambler. Remember how your brain isn't done growing yet? A lot of stressed teens are significantly depressed and have very low self-esteem that gets boosted when they gamble and win. They find this boost gratifying. Unfortunately, they can get hooked on gambling, start to lose, and become more depressed and stressed.

Sex

Most teens will face the question of whether or not to become sexually active and when. For some, there may be conflicts between what one has been brought up to believe about sexual relationships and what one is being encouraged to do by potential sexual partners. This can create a tremendous amount of stress. Teens who are consciously deciding about becoming sexually active should think things through, choose a caring partner, and always use protection.

Sometimes having sex can have unintended health consequences. According to the Centers for Disease Control and Prevention, half of the twenty million new STD cases reported each year come from people aged fifteen to twenty-four. Twenty-one percent of new HIV cases are from those ages thirteen to twenty-four. While teen pregnancy rates in the United States are down, 210,000 teens had babies in 2016. Always remember that condoms, which teens report using only 46 percent of the time, can help you to have safer sex.

Sexual assault is also a very serious stressor. You have the right to say no to having sex at any time, even if you have said yes before. And if someone says no to you during a sexual encounter, you must stop immediately. According to RAINN, the Rape,

Actor Christina Ricci talks with former representative Jane Harman during an event for RAINN (Rape, Abuse & Incest National Network). RAINN helps those who have experienced abuse.

Abuse & Incest National Network, women ages sixteen to nineteen are four times more likely than the rest of the general population to be the victim of rape, attempted rape, or sexual assault. Sexual abuse can have serious consequences for one's life and mental health, including an increased likelihood of abusing drugs, and experiencing PTSD and depression. There are resources available to help, some of which are listed at the end of this book. Also consider talking to a parent or trusted friend.

CHAPTER FIVE

Getting Control Over Your Stress

So now you know what stress does to your body, and how it can make you sick. You also know distructive ways to deal with feeling overwhelmed. But how do you cope? Here are some ideas to help you get stress under control in a healthy way.

Psychologist and author David Elkind says that each person has a finite amount of energy to devote to life's activities. If one expends a lot of energy dealing with stressors, then there is a lot less to expend on activities that lead to a satisfying life. The trick is to find positive ways to respond to stress—those that will expend the least energy—so that there is plenty left to build a great life.

The Importance of Self-Esteem

Self-image is the way you see yourself in relation to others. Are you satisfied with your physical appearance? How's your personality? Do you like yourself and think others like you, too? Improving your self-image is the first step in having a positive "sense of self."

The next step is to develop a healthy self-esteem. Self-esteem is the opinion you have of yourself based on your attitude about many factors in your life. These include your value as a person, your achievements, your purpose in life, your strengths and weaknesses, and your independence.

Feeling Better About Yourself

So how do you improve your self-image and boost your self-esteem? One possible first step to improving self-image is to list things you like about yourself. As you do that, you will undoubtedly think of things you do not like about yourself. It is very important, however, to question whether your view of those things is accurate, or whether you are being too hard on yourself. For instance, you may be very critical of your appearance, not because you are unattractive but because you are comparing yourself to popular images of people on TV or in magazines. If, realistically, changes need to be made to improve your self-image, start with easy ones such as changing your hair or getting a few new clothes. Take a positive approach to things that are harder to change, like your weight. Think of them as challenges instead of obstacles.

As you improve your self-image, you will find that you are also strengthening your self-esteem. Here are a few other suggestions to help you improve self-esteem.

Use Positive Speech

If you stop to think about it, you are constantly having mental conversations with yourself. If you bad-mouth yourself in these conversations, you may soon believe you are a bad person. Put a positive spin on your mental conversations rather than a negative one. For instance, if you have done badly on a test at school, instead of saying to yourself, "You dummy, how could you be so stupid?" think, "Wow, that was a hard test. I really need to study harder for the next one."

Be tolerant of your own mistakes. Nobody is perfect. It is easy to be excessively critical of yourself, especially when things are not going well. Mistakes happen, but the key is to admit when you make one, learn from it, then let it go.

Acknowledge Your Accomplishments

Most teens feel that passing their driver's license test or getting really high grades is a big accomplishment, but you should also recognize your smaller accomplishments. Getting to school on time or receiving a compliment at work are also things that should matter. Make a daily list of those things, even if they don't seem very important. By recognizing your accomplishments, you begin to understand that you have self-worth.

Be Assertive

Being able to let others know what you think and feel is important. After all, what you have to say is just as important as what others have to say. As a teen, you may think your parents and other adults do not want to know what you think or what is important to you, but most adults welcome conversations with teens. Having a give-and-take conversation with kids is one of the joys of parenthood. Say what you think, but also listen to others and respect their opinions.

Spend time with people who value you. Listen to what they say about you. People you choose to be around are often mirrors of how you feel about yourself. If others are constantly putting you down, you're running with the wrong crowd!

Time to Take Control

With your self-image buffed and your self-esteem maximized, you are ready to deal with stress and make it work for you. Here are a few steps that will help you to take control.

It is definitely easier said than done, but thinking positively about yourself can have a big effect on your self-esteem. Try being your biggest cheerleader and see what happens.

Define the Problem

Know that you cannot eliminate all stress from your life. Who can? Define your individual list of major stressors. Take the time to analyze your day. Write down how you spent your time, who you interacted with, and how you responded to situations. It is especially important to note your feelings—were you happy, sad, or infuriated? Keep track of these things for several days, then set aside an hour or so to analyze your notes. You may be surprised to find out what did or did not cause you stress. Once you know what your major stressors are, you can formulate a plan to deal with them.

Learn to Manage Your Time

One of the main stressors identified by teens is the lack of time to do everything that is expected of them. You're being pulled in a million different directions—school, work, extracurricular activities, friends, family—it's exhausting just thinking about it! But if you exercise good time management and work to schedule activities you have to do, as well as those you want to do, it can help you keep control of your schedule.

List those daily and weekly activities that you know you have to do. For instance, if there is a

Keeping close track of your commitments can help you to know what's coming—and what you should say no to. A well-kept schedule can help you manage stress.

science fair project due on Friday, note down the date and the times during the week that you are setting aside to work on the project. Always list your routine commitments, like classes, band practice, student council meetings, or after-school jobs. After you get all of the "must-dos" into your schedule, start filling in uncommitted time slots with things you should do, like getting a head start on research for a term paper or volunteering to help with your kid brother's school carnival. You are in control of this schedule, so build time into it for everything: alone time, family time, recreational time, or even time to sleep. Keep this schedule with you so you can always update it.

Realistically, no schedule will ever be perfect. Your friends will still call to chat or want you to go out at inopportune times, and occasionally you will rebel against the regimentation you are imposing on yourself. If you stick with it most of the time, though, you will find even an incredibly busy schedule to be much less stressful than it was before. You are in control.

Learn to Say No

Let's say you've got your schedule timed down to the minute, and you're still stressed and overwhelmed. Then it's time to learn to say no to some commitments. Do you sometimes agree to do a lot of things you don't want to do simply because you think you should? To some extent that is unavoidable. For instance, your mother may have suggested that you volunteer to help with your brother's school carnival. You don't really want to do it, but it is important to your mother and your brother, and they are important to you—so you do it. On the other hand, if you're asked to be on a committee to plan an activity you have no interest in, you don't have to say yes. Start thinking about your priorities. What is most important to you? Saving up for a new phone, acing your history test, or maybe that speech you have to make at the next United Nations meeting. Prioritize your life and proceed accordingly. If you need help figuring out what's most important, it can be time to call in a parent or friend to help you decide. Guard your time—no one else will.

Practice and Prepare

One of the most stressful things you can do is approach an event without preparation. For example, perhaps a requirement for your history class is that you give a brief talk on a historical subject of your choice. You've chosen to discuss Lewis and Clark and their voyage of discovery. You know the material well, but the thought of presenting it puts you in a panic. Practice your talk in front of a mirror beforehand. Give the talk to your parents, a friend, or even your dog. You will find that because you have practiced and are prepared, you have harnessed your stress and made it work for you. When the time comes to present your subject, you will be more relaxed than if you had not prepared.

Finish What You Start

With your busy schedule, you may find that you never quite finish anything to your satisfaction. Projects or chores that you started weeks ago are still hanging over your head while you try to deal with more urgent matters. Eventually, everything piles up and you may begin to feel overwhelmed. You can minimize stress by making a concerted effort to finish each project or chore as it comes along. Break big chores into a group of smaller tasks that can be completed in a reasonable amount of time. Soon, the entire project will be done. You will get a great deal of satisfaction from actually finishing something you've started.

You've heard it a million times because it's true! Eating healthy and drinking a lot of water will make you feel better. Taking care of yourself is the first step to managing stress.

Be Good to Your Body

Coping with outside stressors if you are physically stressed is very difficult. These are the "big three" of staying physically healthy:

1. **Eat right and stay hydrated.** Stress reactions require your body to expend tremendous amounts of energy. You get the fuel for these reactions from food, but grabbing a quick bite when you're busy could mean you're eating a lot of fast food, snacks, and sodas. These foods are high in calories, fats, and caffeine, and they're low in basic nutrients, vitamins, and minerals. Your body isn't getting what it needs to help you fuel your stress reactions, and it's being overwhelmed with things that may worsen these reactions, so take the time to eat well-rounded meals. Your body also needs water to keep all your systems working. If you're dehydrated, you may feel tired, cranky, or weepy, and can experience nausea and lightheadedness. Simply drinking water can make all of these symptoms disappear.
2. **Get enough sleep.** Sleep deprivation problems can add to the stressors in your life. People

usually need seven or eight hours of sleep a night, but most teens don't get that much. Melatonin, a hormone that regulates sleeping and waking patterns, is produced later at night in teens than it is in younger kids and adults. Teens tend to fall asleep later at night and, if their schedules allow, sleep later in the morning. However, teens who fall asleep after midnight

Exercise is another great way to manage stress. Why not try a class with friends, that way you can hang out and get your heart rate going at the same time?

may still have to be up early for school, so over time they may become sleep deprived. Sleep deprivation leads to impairment in judgment and the ability to think. It may also lead to impairment of motor skills and reaction times. This can have serious consequences, especially if sleep-deprived teens are driving.

3. **Get plenty of exercise.** Exercise has three major benefits in helping to control stress. First, it helps to counterbalance the added caloric intake that is common in kids on the run. By expending some of those extra calories in physical activity, teens are less likely to gain weight and will have an easier time maintaining positive self-images. Second of all, exercise can decrease stress by causing increased production of endorphins, or natural opioids, in the brain. This gives a natural high that counterbalances the lows of stress. The third benefit of exercise is that you'll have an outlet for all the pent-up energy that stress produces. By expending this energy productively, you are less likely to react impulsively and violently in situations.

CHAPTER SIX

When It's Time to Get Help

Stressors are everywhere. Most of the time these problems can be handled with little trouble, but sometimes a difficulty cannot be handled alone. But there is help available. All you need to do is ask.

Earl Hipp, clinical psychologist and author of *Fighting Invisible Tigers: A Stress-Management Guide for Teens*, says that the most challenging thing to do in dealing with severe stress is to admit that help is needed. This is not a sign of weakness; it is a sign of a very strong person. Dr. Donna M. Callaghan, a professor at Widener University, says kids often want help but don't know how or whom to ask. She suggests that one ask oneself these questions before reaching out to someone:

- Why do I think I need help?
- How severe are my stressors?
- Are my stressors day-to-day problems, like trying to manage time or meeting obligations?
- Are my stressors bigger things, such as trying to cope with life transitions or peer pressure?
- Are my stressors truly traumatic, like being raped or being hooked on drugs?
- What kind of help do I need?

By clarifying the answers to these questions, one will be more likely to ask the right person for help. You will also be able to express your needs more clearly when you do ask for help.

Talk to Someone

Once you have decided that you need help, the challenge is to reach out and talk to someone. Who will listen and not be judgmental? Who can help? Although it may be hard to believe at times, you are not alone. Others can be there for you if you ask. Care and support may be found among friends and family. If you seek an ear outside of your circle, school counselors, therapists, and support groups can be great resources.

Parents

Those of you who can comfortably talk to your parents are truly lucky. You know that you can bring even the most stressful situation to them and be

Eating dinner with your family and talking about your day can help you feel connected to each other. You can share problems and concerns or just update each other on your lives. Try it!

assured of getting sound advice. However, teens can also be stressed by conflicts with their parents. And the inability to communicate with a parent can also create conflicts. The reasons for these communication problems are varied. Ironically, the very fact that you are maturing may be one of the prime problems.

Dr. Judith Rapaport from the National Institute of Mental Health observed 145 kids from childhood into their teen years, using magnetic resonance imaging (MRIs), or special brain scans, to see what happened to their brains as they aged. She found that at about the same time the kids reached puberty, their brain scans showed enlargement of the frontal lobes. This part of the brain is the area where planning, reasoning, and impulse control occur. With various psychological test methods, she found that these kids—most of whom were teens by this point—had improved their problem-solving skills, demonstrated the ability to make responsible choices, and were already developing their own beliefs and values. In other words, they were maturing.

"So what?" you ask. "How does all this relate to talking or not talking to my parents?" In an article about teens talking to parents and other adults, the authors point out that while you are gaining confidence in yourself and your ability to resolve problems, your parents are having a hard time realizing that you aren't the little kid whom they have been making decisions for all these years. The disparity between how you see yourself and how your parents see you can lead to disagreements. In some cases, you may decide that you simply can't talk with them, and they may decide the same thing.

When you run into stressors that you can't handle alone, in spite of your new maturity, it is frequently hard to reopen new lines of communication with your parents. The article suggested this strategy: define the issues you want to discuss with your parents. You may find it helpful to actually write down the most important points you want to cover so you don't forget them. Limit these to three or four main topics. Be clear that you have an important issue you want to discuss. Schedule your talk for a specific time when you will have their undivided attention. Finally, write down your thoughts and give them to your parents before the discussion.

Family and Friends

There may be times when you simply cannot talk with your parents. Hopefully there are other adults available in your life. Consider, do you have a favorite teacher, coach, member of a religious group, grandparent, aunt, or uncle can listen and provide comfort? They can also know when to steer you to a professional who can help.

You may even turn to your friends. Real friends are those who will tell you what you need to hear, not what you want to hear. If you are scared, depressed, confused, or desperate to escape from a situation or habit that has gotten out of hand, choose a friend you trust who will be brutally honest with you and talk to that person. This friend may already know a lot about what you are feeling.

Support Groups

One of the most effective ways of dealing with a problem is to meet with other people who have experienced or are experiencing the same thing.

These support groups may be started by two or three people who work through problems together. Later, as the group expands, the original members provide guidance to newer members. They may call on psychologists, physicians, or other professionals to give help when needed. However, the main advantage of this type of group lies in knowing that others understand the problems you are having because they've all been there. You can find support groups online. Many have hotlines or online chat options that you can use if you feel desperate. They honestly care and can help you deal with a crisis, as well as continue to provide support as long as you need it.

Counselors and Psychotherapists

A school counselor's job is to help kids cope with problems. They have special training in many areas, so they aren't limited to helping with school issues. Counselors are also knowledgeable about the availability of support groups or therapists they can refer you to should you need it.

Sometimes a teen will have problems so troubling that friends and/or parents feel unable to give the teen adequate help. At that point, the teen may have

If stress becomes overwhelming, help is available. Try talking to a trusted adult or your guidance counselor. Therapy can be a great tool to manage stress.

to see a psychotherapist. A therapist is professionally trained to help with emotional and behavioral problems. It's the goal of a therapist to help teens learn about themselves, discover ways to overcome troubling feelings and behaviors, and develop good coping skills.

Supplemental Help?

Experts in stress management have written books, made videos, and started websites on topics ranging from time management to relaxation techniques and everything in between. Perhaps you would like suggestions about visual imaging, meditation, yoga, or aromatherapy. Many of these books, tapes, and DVDs can be found in your public library.

There are many websites dedicated to helping one deal with stress and stress management that are available to check out, but do so with caution. When you are experiencing stress overload, you may be particularly vulnerable to exploitation by those who advertise quick

(continued on the next page)

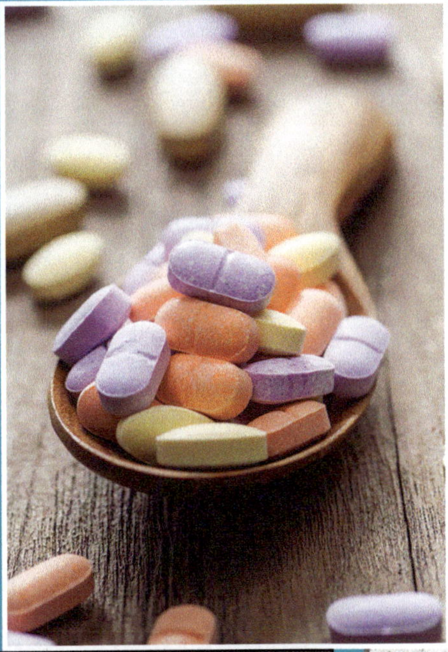

Not all vitamins do what the commercials say. Be careful when taking supplements. It's always a good idea to check with a doctor before taking something new.

(continued from the previous page)

fixes for all of your woes. If it sounds too good to be true, it probably is.

Be particularly cautious about trying natural medications or supplements advertised to relieve stress. Many of these products contain chemicals in amounts that are potentially toxic. There is no agency regulating the companies that make these products, so their efficacy, potency, and purity may not be known. Ask your doctor or therapist about any type of medication or supplement before taking it. You may save yourself a lot of money, not to mention your life.

The approach a therapist uses depends on a teen's individual needs, but it always includes listening, exchanging information, building trust, and respecting confidentiality. In some instances, a therapist may recommend and prescribe medication to help a teen through a crisis. Few require long-term drug therapy. Once a teen and his or her therapist have developed a workable plan for dealing with stressors, it will be up to the teen to implement the

Spending time with friends, simply talking about your day or taking a stroll to get coffee, can be a great stress reliever. Getting out into the sunshine can also help you feel better.

plan with the therapist's help. The coping skills they learn will benefit them for life.

The teen years can be a time of major life crises. You are experiencing many physical changes that can be stressful. You are developing your own beliefs and values. You are faced with the challenges of deciding your future educational goals, where to take relationships, and how to respond to endless demands on your time. You are also living in an era of unprecedented technological expansion that is mind-boggling. Is there any wonder that you are stressed?

As you have seen, there are many ways to cope with stress. Perhaps some of the positive coping mechanisms presented here will prove helpful to you. Underlying all of these is one recurring theme—you are not alone. Regardless of what your stressors are and how hopeless things may seem, talking with someone will help, so give it a try.

10 Great Questions to Ask a Doctor About Stress

1. Do most teens know when they are under too much stress? If so, how? What are the symptoms?
2. Could I have an underlying medical condition that adds to my stress symptoms?
3. Could my stress make my medical problems worse?
4. Are there any tests to determine my cause(s) of stress?
5. If untreated, could stress cause more serious conditions to occur?
6. Can exercise and adequate sleep really help me manage my stress?
7. What lifestyle changes can I make to decrease stress?
8. What substances should I stay away from if I feel really stressed? Why?
9. Are there videos, books, or brochures that contain useful information about my symptoms?
10. Would I benefit from seeing a psychologist or psychiatrist?

Glossary

activist Someone who works to change the world, often socially or politically, via protests or other actions.

adrenaline A hormone made in the adrenal glands in response to stress.

adrenocorticotropic hormone (ACTH) Produced by the pituitary gland, ACTH instructs the adrenal glands to produce cortisol.

autonomic nervous system Also known as the involuntary nervous system, it controls the body's ability to relax and digest and is in charge of the flight-or-flight response.

blood alcohol content (BAC) The percentage of alcohol in a person's blood stream.

cholesterol A white, fatty, crystalline alcohol that is found in bile, egg yolks, and other foods and in nerve tissues.

corticotropin-releasing hormone (CRH) Made by the hypothalamus in response to stress, CRH tells the pituitary gland to make ACTH.

cortisol The main stress hormone, cortisol increases glucose in the bloodstream and helps with the fight-or-flight response, among other things.

depression The absence of cheer or hope; emotional dejection.

endorphins Chemicals produced in the brain that can cause euphoria or other positive feelings.

fight or flight Physiological changes in the body resulting from stress.

gambling To play a game for money or other stakes.

glucose A simple sugar that is the main energy source for body reactions. Many glucose molecules are combined and stored in the liver and other tissues as glycogen. When needed, glycogen is broken down into smaller glucose molecules.

herpes simplex virus (HSV) The virus that causes herpes and sometimes causes small blisters on the mouth and lips, also called cold sores.

HIV The human immunodeficiency virus can develop into acquired immunodeficiency syndrome (AIDS) if left untreated.

hormone A chemical substance produced in one place in the body that is carried through the bloodstream to another part of the body where it causes some type of reaction.

hypothalamus The region of the brain that controls the autonomic nervous system by regulating functions such as sleep cycles, appetite, and body temperature.

magnetic resonance imaging (MRI) An imaging method developed in the 1980s that is well adapted for studying the nervous system. The technique involves the use of magnetic fields rather than radiation to create images.

physiology The study of the function of the organs and other body parts during life.

platelet A tiny, colorless, disc-shaped structure found in blood that, when disrupted, initiates the clotting of blood.

syndrome A group of signs and symptoms that occur together and characterize a disease or disorder.

toxic Poisonous.

For More Information

American Institute of Stress
220 Adams Drive
Suite 280 #224
Weatherford, TX 76086 USA
(682) 239-6823
Email: info@stress.org
Website: http://www.stress.org
Facebook: @aistress
Twitter: @AIS_StressNews
The institute is a clearinghouse for information on stress. It has a large library and has reprints available.

Canadian Institute of Stress
The Vital Corporation
3300 Bloor Street W Suite 650
West Tower
Toronto, ON M8X 2X2
Canada
(416) 236-4218
Website: http://www.stresscanada.org
Email: Info@stresscanada.org
The institute was founded by Dr. Hans Selye and is involved with research into the causes and

treatments for stress. It provides educational programs, as well as individual counseling.

Canadian Mental Health Association
250 Dundas Street West, Suite 500
Toronto, ON M5T 2Z5
Canada
(416) 484-7756
Email: info@cmha.ca
Website: http://www.cmha.ca
Twitter: @ CMHA_NTL
Instagram: @cmhanational
This is the oldest voluntary organization in Canada. It is a nationwide organization of volunteers that promotes mental health with advocacy, education, research, and service.

Children of the Night
14530 Sylvan Street
Van Nuys, CA 91411
(818) 808-4474
Hotline: (800) 551-1800
Website: http://www.childrenofthenight.org
Twitter: @cotnight

Facebook and Instagram: @ childrenofthenightinc
This organization provides help for runaways or other children who are in crisis situations.

Crisis Text Line
19 West 2st Street, Eighth Floor
New York, NY 10010-6853
Text HOME to 741741 in the United States
Text HOME to 686868 in Canada
Website: http://www.crisistextline.org
Twitter, Facebook, and Instagram: @CrisisTextLine
Formed by DoSomething.org, the Crisis Text Line was created to help anyone in crisis, at any time. Those in Canada and America can access a trained crisis counselor twenty-four hours a day via text message.

National Institute of Mental Health Office of Science Policy, Planning, and Communications
6001 Executive Boulevard, Room 6200
MSC 9663
Bethesda, MD 208992-9663
(301) 443-4513
(866) 615-6464

Email: nimhinfo@nih.gov
Website: http://www.nimh.nih.gov
Facebook and Twitter: @NIMHgov
The institute is the branch of the National Institutes of Health concerned with mental health. Evaluation and treatment, as well as education and research, are its goals.

RAINN: Rape, Abuse & Incest National Network, National Sexual Assault Hotline
1220 L Street NW
Washington, DC 20005
(800) 656-4673
Website: http://www.rainn.org
Facebook: @RAINN01
Twitter and Instagram: @RAINN
RAINN and its national hotline are dedicated to helping those in need after a sexual assault. Survivors can call or online chat twenty-four hours a day.

For Further Reading

Anderson, Laurie Halse. *The Impossible Knife of Memory*. New York, NY: Viking, 2014.

Bellfield, Annie. *Stressed Out Girl? How to Deal*. New York, NY: Enslow, 2014.

Bernstein, Jeffrey. *Mindfulness for Teen Worry : Quick & Easy Strategies To Let Go Of Anxiety, Worry, & Stress*. Oakland, CA: Instant Help Publications, 2017.

Clark, Travis. *A Stressed Out Guy's Guide: How to Deal*. New York, NY: Enslow, 2014.

Kaplan, A. E. *Grendel's Guide to Love and War*. New York, NY: Knopf, 2017.

Morgan, Nicola. *The Teenage Guide to Stress*. London, UK: Walker Books, 2014.

Rissman, Rebecca. *Yoga for Your Mind and Body: A Teenage Practice for a Healthy, Balanced Life*. North Mankato, MN: Capstone Press, 2015.

Staley, Erin. *Defeating Stress and Anxiety*. New York, NY: Rosen Publishing, 2016.

Stebner, Beth. *Stop, Breathe, Chill: Meditations for A Less Stressful, More Awesome Life*. Avon, MA: Adams Media, 2016.

Way, Jennifer, and Sara Van Duyne. *What You Can Do About Stress and Anxiety*. New York, NY: Enslow Publishing, 2016.

Bibliography

Cannon, Walter Bradford. *The Way of an Investigator: A Scientist's Experiences in Medical Research.* New York, NY: Norton, 1984.

Denizet-Lewis, Benoit. "Why Are More American Teenagers Than Ever Suffering from Anxiety." *New York Times,* October 11, 2017. https://www.nytimes.com/2017/10/11/magazine/why-are-more-american-teenagers-than-ever-suffering-from-severe-anxiety.html.

Graf, Nikki. "A Majority of U.S. Teens Fear a Shooting Could Happen at Their School, and Most Parents Share Their Toncern." "Fact Tank: News in the Numbers." Pew Research Center, April 18, 2018. http://www.pewresearch.org/fact-tank/2018/04/18/a-majority-of-u-s-teens-fear-a-shooting-could-happen-at-their-school-and-most-parents-share-their-concern.

Hedegaard, Holly. "Suicide Rates in the United States Continue to Increase." National Center for Health Statistics Data Brief No. 309, June 2018. https://www.cdc.gov/nchs/products/databriefs/db309.htm.

Hipp, Earl. *Fighting Invisible Tigers: A Stress-Management Guide for Teens.* Minneapolis, MN: Free Spirit Publishing, Inc., 1995.

Jackson, Sandra L. "Hypertension Among Youths—United States 2001—2006." *Morbidity and Mortality Weekly Report*, July 13, 2018. https://www.cdc.gov/mmwr/volumes/67/wr/mm6727a2.htm?s_cid=mm6727a2_w.

Johnston, Lloyd D. "Monitoring Future National Survey Results on Drug Use 1975–2017: Key Findings on Adolescent Drug Use." National Institute on Drug Abuse at The National Institutes of Health." http://www.monitoringthefuture.org/pubs/monographs/mtf-overview2017.pdf.

Mazziotta, Julie. "Teen Stress Is on the Rise: Why It's a Major Problem, and How You Can Help." *People*, May 14, 2018. https://people.com/health/teen-stress-rising-what-to-do.

National Center for Health Statistics, Centers for Disease Control and Prevention "Mortality in the United States, 2016." December 2017. https://www.cdc.gov/nchs/products/databriefs/db293.htm.

National Center for Injury Prevention and Control Division of Violence Prevention, Centers for Disease Control and Prevention."Preventing Teen Dating Violence," 2017. https://www.cdc

.gov/violenceprevention/pdf/tdv-factsheet.pdf.

National Institute of Alcohol Abuse and Alcoholism. "Underage Drinking Fact Sheet." February 2017. https://pubs.niaaa.nih.gov/publications/UnderageDrinking/UnderageFact.htm.

National Institutes of Health. "Stress System Malfunction Could Lead to Serious, Life-Threatening Disease." NIH Backgrounder, September 9, 2002. http://www. nih.gov/news/pr/sept2002/nichd-09.htm.

New York University College of Nursing. "NYU Study Examines Top High School Students' Stress and Coping Mechanisms." August 11, 2015. https://www.nyu.edu/about/news-publications/news/2015/august/nyu-study-examines-top-high-school-students-stress-and-coping-mechanisms.html.

Patchin, Justin W. "2015 Cyberbullying Data." Cyberbullying Research Center, May 1, 2015. https://cyberbullying.org/2015-data.

Sam Houston State University. "Juvenile Gang Members in US Top 1 million, New Study Finds." *ScienceDaily*, February 12, 2015. http://

www.sciencedaily.com/releases/2015/02/150212131817.htm

Schrobsdorff, Susanna. "Teen Depression and Anxiety: Why the Kids Are Not Alright." *Time*, October 27, 2016. http://time.com/4547322/american-teens-anxious-depressed-overwhelmed.

Science Daily. "Research Reveals Likely Connection Between Early-Life Stress and Teenage Mental Health Problems." November 16, 2005. https://news.ohsu.edu/2005/11/16/ohsu-research-reveals-likely-connection-between-early-life-stress-and-mental-health-problems-during-the-teenage-years.

Seaward, Brian, and Linda Bartlett. *Hot Stones and Funny Bones: Teens Helping Teens Cope with Stress and Anger*. Deerfield Beach, FL: HCI, 2002.

Sluke, Sara Jane, and Vanessa Torres. *The Complete Idiot's Guide to Dealing with Stress for Teens*. Indianapolis, IN: Alpha Books, 2002.

United States Department of Health and Human Services, Administration for Children and Families, Administration on Children, Youth and Families, Children's Bureau. "Child Maltreatment Survey, 2012." 2013. https://www.acf.hhs.gov/sites/default/files/cb/cm2012.pdf.

United States Department of Health and Human Services, Centers for Disease Control and Prevention, National Center for Chronic Disease Prevention and Health Promotion, Office on Smoking and Health. "The Health Consequences of Smoking—50 Years of Progress: A Report of the Surgeon General," 2014. https://www.cdc.gov/tobacco/data_statistics/sgr/50th-anniversary/index.htm.

Index

A

activity load, 41–42
adaptive/resistance stage, 18–19
addiction, 55–57
adrenocorticotrophic hormone (ACTH), 16
alarm stage, 18
alcohol abuse, 60–63
American Psychological Association, 39
anxiety, 4, 7, 22, 29, 33

C

Centers for Disease Control and Prevention (CDC), 25, 26, 29, 30, 46, 60, 66
common causes of stress
  current events, 52–54
  family issues, 35–37
  online issues, 50–52
  school stress, 37– 43
  social issues, 43–50
corticotropin-releasing hormone (CRH), 15–16, 18
cortisol, 16, 17, 22–24, 29–30, 33–34
counselors, 89–90, 92, 94
cyberbullying, 50–51

D

dating violence, 44–47
depression, 29–32, 60, 63, 68
diet, 79–80
divorce, 36–37
drug abuse, 63–65

E

effects on the body, 12–15
Elkind, David, 69
exercise, 82
exhaustion stage, 19

F

fight-or-flight response, 10

G

gambling, 65
gangs, 48–49
gastrointestinal system, 24–25
general adaptation

syndrome (GAD), 18–19
genetics, 20
González, Emma, 53
Graf, Nikki, 42
Gurwitch, Robin H., 39

H

Hedegaard, Holly, 30
Heyland, Alison, 4
high blood pressure, 25–27
Higher Education Research Institute, 7
Hipp, Earl, 83
HIV, 66
hypertension, 25

I

illness, 37
immune system, 22–24
irritable bowel syndrome (IBS), 25

J

Jackson, Sandra, 25

L

La Guardia, Tommy, 5
Leonard, Noelle, 40
Luthar, Suniya, 4

M

MRIs, 86
myths, 20–21

N

National Institute of Mental Health, 86
National Institute on Alcohol Abuse and Alcoholism, 60
National Institute on Drug Abuse, 64
National Suicide Prevention Lifeline, 32

O

obesity, 29

P

parent expectations, 38–39
Parkland Florida, 53

peptic ulcers, 24–25
positive speech, 71–72
pregnancy, 66
psychotherapists, 89– 90, 92, 94
PTSD, 68
Pyrooz, David, 48

R

Rapaport, Judith, 86
rape, 46, 66–68, 84
Rape, Abuse & Incest National Network (RAINN), 66–67
reaching out, 84–94
reproductive system, 33–34

S

school shootings, 42–43, 53
Schrobsdorff, Susanna, 4, 5, 7
self-esteem, 70–71
self-image, 49–50, 70–71
Selye, Hans, 9–11, 18
sex, 65–68
sexual abuse, 36
sleep, 80–81
smoking, 57–58
social media, 51–52
STDs, 66
suicide, 29–32, 51, 61
supplements, 91–92
support groups, 88–89

T

time management, 74–76

V

vaping, 59–60

W

weight, 29
Whitlock, Janis, 7
workload, 39–41

Y

Yousafzai, Malala, 53–54

About the Authors

Elissa Thompson is a journalist who has been published in *USA Weekend*, the *Baltimore Sun*, and *In Touch Weekly*, among other publications. Before receiving her master's degree from the University of Maryland, she worked at the Society for Neuroscience, dedicated to better understanding the brain and nervous system.

Linda Bickerstaff is a retired general and peripheral vascular surgeon, as well as a published author of books for children and young adults. Some of Bickerstaff's published credits include *Modern-Day Slavery* (In the News) and *Careers in Nutrition* (Careers in the New Economy).

Photo Credits

Cover Terry Vine/Blend Images/Getty Images; p. 5 © iStockphoto /monkeybusinessimages; p. 6 Steve Dunwell/Photographer's Choice /Getty Images; p. 8 kryzhov/Shutterstock.com; p. 11 John Olson/The LIFE Images Collection/Getty Images; p. 13 sruilk/Shutterstock.com; p. 14 Designua/Shutterstock.com; p. 17 William Perugini/Shutterstock.com; p. 23 Steve Debenport/E+/Getty Images; p. 26 © iStockphoto/AlexRaths; p. 28 ERproductions Ltd/Blend Images/Getty Images; p. 32 National Suicide Prevention Lifeline; p. 38 © iStockphoto/DmitriiSimakov; p. 43 Rhona Wise/AFP/Getty Images; p. 45 FotoShoot/iStock/Getty Images; p. 52 Noam Galai/WireImage/Getty Images; p. 53 NurPhoto/Getty Images; p. 56 Nerthuz/Shutterstock.com; p. 59 Oleg GawriloFF/Shutterstock.com; p. 62 oneinchpunch/Shutterstock.com; p. 67 Kris Connor/WireImage /Getty Images; p. 74 pnDl/Shutterstock.com; p. 75 Andrey Popov /Shutterstock.com; p. 79 stockcreations/Shutterstock.com; p. 81 Sergey Novikov/Shutterstock.com; p. 85 Radius Images/Getty Images; p. 90 Africa Studio/Shutterstock.com; p. 91 1989studio/Shutterstock.com; p. 93 kali9/E+/Getty Images.

Design and Layout: Nicole Russo-Duca; Editor: Elissa Petruzzi; Photo Researcher: Sherri Jackson